EARTH, AIR, FIRE, WATER

A Wreath of Rhymes

LYNNE SARTY PETERSEN

ARPress
ILLUMINATING IDEAS.
EMPOWERING VOICES

ARPress
45 Dan Road Suite 5
Canton MA 02021

Hotline: 1(888) 821-0229
Fax: 1(508) 545-7580

Ordering Information:
Quantity sales. Special discounts are available on quantity purchases by corporations, associations, and others. For details, contact the publisher at the address above.

Printed in the United States of America.

ISBN-13:   Softcover   979-8-89356-472-3
           eBook   979-8-89356-471-6

Library of Congress Control Number: 2024904595

CONTENTS

Earth

Caravan...3

Companion 4

Crossing the Sahara 5

Crystal Journey...6

Desert Horse 7

2-X17-002 10

Grandfather Sun..11

Journey..12

Mountain Madness 13

Naaqah (The Camel) 15

The Merry Maidens 17

The Cellar Hole 18

Walking in the Woods..19

The Temple... 20

The Mountaineer 23

Land Trust...26

The Call to Prayer 27

Fisher-Cat 28

Air

Allahu Akbar 30

Shades 31

Fairy Ring...32

Fortune Teller 33

Magic Carpet Ride 34

Meditation..35

The Messenger..37

Muse 39

On High.. 40

Shadows 41

Shape-Shifting 42

Snowbird... 43

The Book of Time.. 44

The Lace Maker..45

Touching the Sky... 46

Troubadour 47

Vespers.. 49

The Wheel of the Year...50

Fire

Crusade..53

The Battle of the Horns of Hattin...55

Others 57

Spinning Wheel... 60

Poor Knights of the Temple...62

Templar..65

Warrior Monk.. 66

Wise Woman 67

Water

Unknown..70

On Turning Eighty-Six...72

Ode to a Viking 73

Tell Me 74

He 75

Unveiled...76

Sea Song...77

Vernal Pool..78

Goddess 79

Images... 80

Reflections..81

Hecate 83

Soul 84

Spirit.. 86

The Web of Wyrd...87

Wishes..89

Here There be Dragons 90

EARTH, AIR, FIRE, WATER

EARTH

(Black Tents)

The black goat hair tents of the nomad will soon be just a memory
as the Bedouin leave the desert and settle into towns and villages.

Black tents of Arabia – the nomad band.
Tents stretched along the hostile strand.
Like bits of jet across the sand,
Marking home – this no man's land.

Rose-grey mare patiently stands
With camel-hair hobbles,
woven by hands Hardened to life
in these shifting sands.

Her lineage traces across the land,
To centuries ago, in King Solomon's band.
Black tents of Arabia on burning sand,
Camels and horses who quietly stand,
Home for a time – this no man's land.

CARAVAN

Burning sand,
Endless land.
Camel bells ringing,
Tassels swinging,
Caravan.

Rocking, swaying,
Softly braying.
Slow moving days,
Ancient ways,
Caravan.

Companion

My camel walks silently,
Our shadow alongside of me.
It follows along without a sound,
Lying there upon the ground.
A constant companion at my side,
Quiet company as I ride.
Heat, dust, the sun's bright glare,
I quickly turn but it's still there.
Hours pass and it grows taller,
Or has this desert made me smaller.

CROSSING THE SAHARA

The caravan moves slowly on,
From daybreak till the sun is gone.
Plodding, plodding across the sand,
Slowly traversing this desolate land.

Now the dunes are rolling by,
Dun colored under an azure sky.
Then we reach the rocky plain,
And the colors change once again.

Black sand crunches as we go,
The miles roll by, but, oh so slow!
Like a kaleidoscope shifting once more,
And nothing is as it was before.

The sand is now a muted green,
Weathered copper that's rarely seen.
Hills in the distance now seem like coal,
As slowly we pass another goal.

The dunes now have a pumpkin hue,
Soon Erg Chebbi is behind us too.
The colors change, the image shifts,
Into blowing sand and endless drifts.

Always changing, yet always the same,
Rolling sand hills that bear no name.
Changing pictures turning around,
Like an old movie, one without sound.

The camels slowly, slowly plod on,
Till azure sky and sun are gone.
The shadows are long in fading light,
And the desert slowly slips into night.

CRYSTAL JOURNEY

Clear quartz crystal, shining bright,
Bathe me with your clear, cool light.
Take me to lands far away,
Just to visit, not to stay.
Show me sights my eyes can't see,
Show me now, what's meant to be.
Tell me things from long ago,
That in my heart, I really know.
I'll journey with you far away,
To see reflections of today.

The Arabian horse was the most valuable possession of the desert nomad. Only on horseback was he safe from raiding war parties. Gray was the preferred color as it symbolized victory, with rose gray (gray on chestnut) very common. Only the mares were ridden as they would not betray their presence to an enemy by making noise. Life was harsh with horses galloping 20 or 30 miles across the desert with no food except a few dates and some camel's milk. Only the hardiest survived and bloodlines tracing back into antiquity were jealously guarded and kept "asil" or pure.

DESERT HORSE

Rose-grey mare
With your tassels so gay,
How many miles
Have you traveled today?

Over the dunes
Of scorching sand,
Miles and miles
Of endless land.

Desert horse
Of the Bedouin tribe
Constantly moving,
Your foal at your side.

Rose-grey mare
As you stop for the night,
A few dried dates,
But only a bite.

It's all your
Desert family can share,
A little milk
The camels can spare.

Then up with the
Sun and moving again,
Dreaming of battles
Your tribe must win.

Another oasis,
The journey's begun,
Under the glare
Of the desert sun.

Mile after mile,
No water or rest,
But in your veins
The blood of the best.

Rose-grey mare
With your tassels so gay,
How many miles
Have you traveled today?

2-XI7-OO2

The rats are red
So Alice said
As she peered thru
The looking glass.
But pigs are pink
So don't you think
They should be in
The higher class?
The Hatter Mad
Said it's too bad
'Cuz rats are never red.
But the Cheshire Cat
Grinned at that
Why bother
They're all dead!

GRANDFATHER SUN

The earth is my mother, my sister, my lover.
The sky is my father, my guardian, my brother.
Grandfather sun lights the day, shows the way.
Grandmother moon lights the night, calms my fright.

The river that flows
The wild wind that blows
The stars in the night
The hawk high in flight

My brothers, my lovers
We are one
We are one
Grandfather sun.

JOURNEY

I hear the call to another land
Where camels plod across the sand.
I need to hear the call to prayer, where
"Salaam Alicum" is the greeting there.
Where rolling dunes keep changing hue
And graceful minarets pierce the blue
Of dazzling, endless, azure skies
Reflected in a lover's eyes.
I want to hear the ney flute's sound
As Sufi's dance and twirl around.
Where soft, plush carpets hide the floor
And bright blue eyes adorn the door
To keep all evil far away
And banish jinn who fear the day.
A land of magic and simple grace,
That binds me fast with chains of lace.

MOUNTAIN MADNESS

"Wither thou goest, I will go"
To climb this mountain robed in snow.
The sentinel trees quietly stand;
Not even a sound in this wonderland.

Everything muffled in mounds of white,
A fairyland fantasy fills my sight.
The Canada jays take food from my hand,
And silently fold their wings to land.

The trail gets steeper at each twist;
I tighten the ice axe around my wrist.
Higher and higher we wind around,
Ice and snow cover the ground.

The trees are smaller and smaller now;
Stunted and gnarled with twisted bough.
"Krumholtz" they're called in the frigid air;
"I'm tired now, are we almost there?"

The summit comes only at a price,
And so as my crampons bite into the ice
I wonder if it's too much to pay;
Should I try again on another day?

My breaths are shorter and shorter here;
I start to feel some pangs of fear.
The tree line now is far behind;
The trail is faint and hard to find.

The wind is strong with icy blast,
I really doubt my strength will last.
You call to me "not much more!"
But my pack is heavy, my muscles sore.

Then mountain madness seizes my soul
And I will not stop still short of my goal.
The rocks are steep; I slowly climb,
And then above me I see the sign.

"Summit" it says, and you reach out a hand
And help me up to proudly stand
On top of the world with a view to see
For miles around; just you and me.

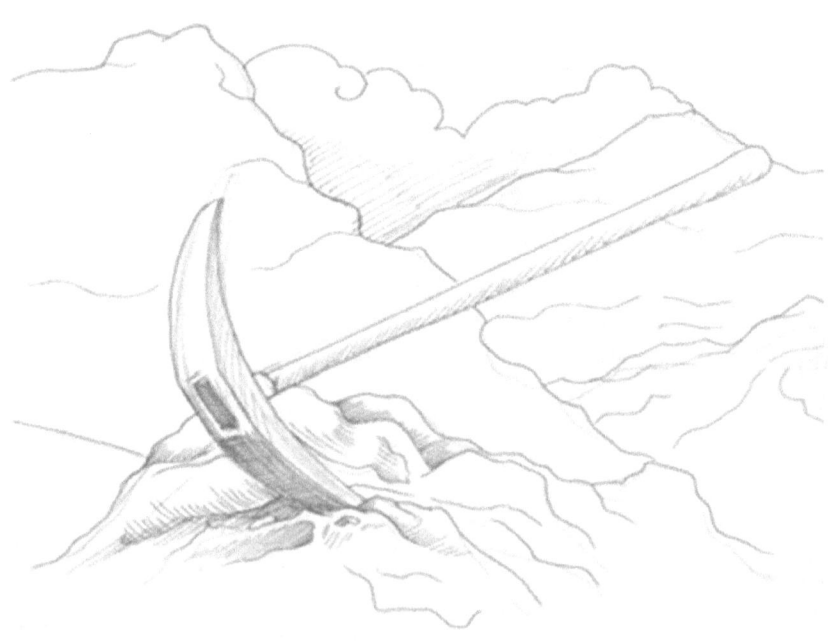

NAAQAH (THE CAMEL)

Ship of the desert, sailing oceans of sand;
The life and the wealth of the nomad band.
Travelling the lands of Scherazade's tales,
Walking with women unseen behind veils.

The Silk Road, the Spice Road, your dusty feet trod.
One foot, then another, you silently plod.
Bells on your harness to keep jinn away,
You traveled by night and rested at day.

From hilltop to wadi, through waves of sand,
A steady course across barren land.
Another oasis, a small brackish well,
Your only relief from a burning hell.

An endless journey that's never done,
Paid for with bones bleached in the sun.
The life of the camel, ship of the sand,
Allah's great gift to a harsh, hostile land.

England is famous for its stone circles, especially Stonehenge on Salisbury Plain. But one of the most beautiful and best-preserved stone circles stands in Cornwall. It's called "The Merry Maidens" and is said to be nineteen maidens turned to stone as a punishment for dancing on a Sunday. The pipers who played for them were also turned to stone and these two unfortunates stand a small distance away from the circle and are called, of course, "The Pipers". This legend was probably set forth by the early Christian Church in order to curb local pagan revelry.

THE MERRY MAIDENS

Standing stones in a ring,
Did you once dance and sing?
Were you once alive like I?
Could you laugh or maybe cry?
Did you once dance around?
While moonlight spilled on the ground?

Lovely maidens dancing there,
With sparkling eyes and flowing hair.
The pipers played with wild delight,
While you danced on Sabbath night.

Now you are forever still,
In your circle on the hill.
But maybe on some Sabbath night,
When the moon is full and bright,
You dance around while pipers play,
And change to stones at break of day.

Written for John Freeman and his sister Jane and the quiet, peaceful woods of their award winning Freeman Family Tree Farm.

THE CELLAR HOLE

A cellar hole hides in the wood
Where once a sturdy farmhouse stood
With barn and dusty fields to sow;
This land was tilled some years ago.
But now the trees grow straight and tall;
The forest has reclaimed it all.
Where's the laughter and the tears
That filled this house through the years?
Now only stones and a well
That hold their counsel, they won't tell
The dramas that unfolded there,
Stories now too old to share.

Quiet now! Can you hear
A lullaby from somewhere near?
Is that the whirr of a spinning wheel?
Or just the rustling leaves I feel?
Far away a rooster crows;
No, it's just the wind that blows.
But listen! There it is again!
A mother calls her children in.
Echoes from another age,
Before time turned the page.

WALKING IN THE WOODS

A dusty path winds through the wood
Winding around as any path should.
Sunlight dappled on the ground,
Deathly silent, not a sound.
A dryad lives in yon gnarled tree.
Shhh! I think she's watching me.
I come across a pool and stone,
A place a fairy would call home.
Close beside a waterfall,
Listen! Hear the raven call?
The woods are home to these and more.
A whiskered face peers out his door,
Beady eyes all alight
He quickly looks and takes flight,
Dashing down his woodsy home
To leave me standing all alone.
I wander on through the dell
Where all the woodland creatures dwell.
To share their realm for a time
Before I must return to mine.

THE TEMPLE

The ruins stand high on a hill,
Ghostly quiet, deathly still.
A column here some marble there,
A stony walkway, perhaps where
Some priestess walked behind the wall,
Hidden from the view of all
Those who came to worship here.
The columns now mute witness bear
To all that came from far away,
Traveling both by night and day,
To bring a sheep or something dear
To offer on the altar here.
To offer up the best they own
In this temple of quiet stone.
Did the gods look down and hear
The true desire in their prayer?

Do they now look down and see
The broken altar and the tree
Where modern pilgrims tie a small
Piece of cloth or in a wall
Tuck a fold of paper between
The stones to remain unseen.
A hidden prayer and offering
For a new God these pilgrims bring.
But those of old dwell here still

In this temple on the hill.
Their day will come once again
And they will walk the land of men.
Until that time the columns stand
A beacon seen across the land.
They watch and wait, deathly still
Ghostly silhouettes on the hill.

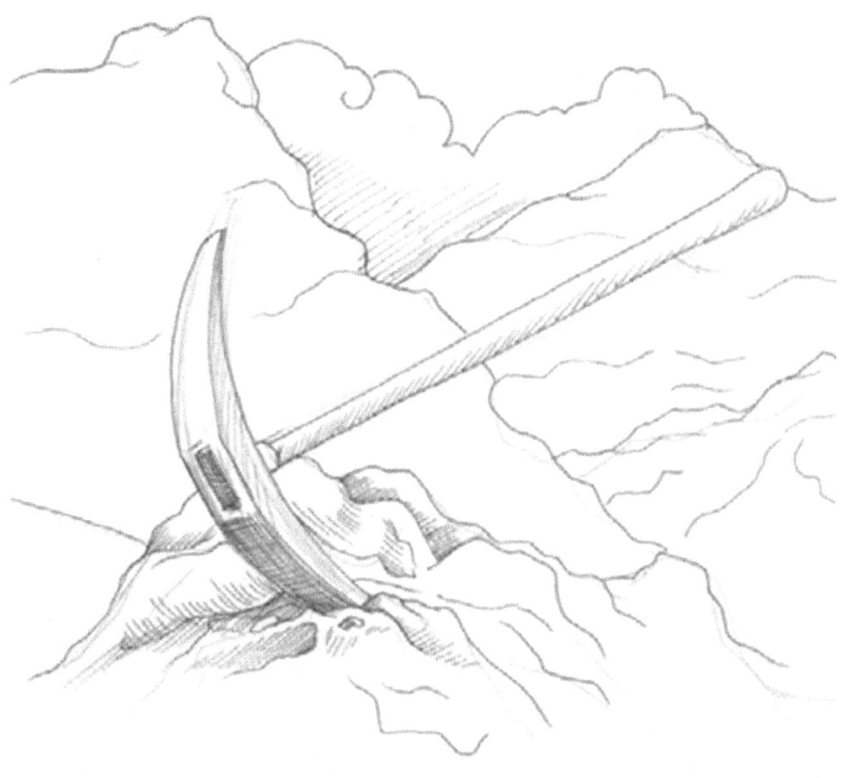

Although the pronoun "he" is used in this poem it is dedicated to the world famous woman mountaineer Lene Gammelgaard whose constant mantra was "to the summit and safe return" and to all the men and women who venture to the world's highest peaks to visit the gods in their ancient home.

THE MOUNTAINEER

(To the Summit and Safely *Home)*

The lofty peaks pierce the sky
Above the clouds gliding by.
Cold blue ice, frozen in time,
Surrounded by rock and rime
And snow drifts sculpted by vicious wind
That creates them only to change again.
Only the brave will climb this high
And even they can't tell you why
They risk their very lives to come
And do what no one else has done.
To come and climb all alone
"To the summit and safely home".
Brave or foolish, who can tell
The difference in this frigid hell,
A place where only gods can dwell.

But the climber stops along the way
At the monastery in order to say
The proper words and to bring
Something to give as an offering
To the gods whose mountain home
He wishes to climb and summit alone.
An ancient monk with wrinkled face
Hobbles forward in order to place

A yellow prayer scarf on his arm
A blessed token to keep him from harm.
The incense smoke swirls round his head
As prayers are offeree to spirits long dead

And rice is thrown from his hand
To scatter far on this frozen land.
The gods demand you honor them
Ere you climb and only then
Will they grant your silent plea
To reach the top and to be
One of the few that go alone
"To the summit and safely home".

The prayers are said, it's time to go
To battle ice, and wind and snow.
He pushes on until he sees
A rainbow of colors in the breeze.
Prayer flags fly against the sky
Near the *chorten* where those who die
Are remembered, stone on stone,
Till a rocky tower has grown;

Warning those who pass it by
"We came to conquer, not to die".
Their spirits whisper in his ear
"Be careful, climber, life is dear.
Take care, or just like us you'll die.
Take care, or just like us you'll lie
Beneath the snow and ice and stone,
In this land that's far from home.
This tower piled with rocks will be
A tribute to your memory!"

And as he passes very near
He tries to quell his rising fear
And leave his doubt far behind
As silently he starts to climb.
But the spirits seem to follow him
As if they need to try again.
And as he inches up the wall
His crampon points stab a small
Clump of ice he prays won't break,

His life the cost of a small mistake.
He pulls himself up to try again
To put his ice axe firmly in
And inch his way up to the sky,
Knowing a slip means he will die.
The shades of all those who tried,
Silent now, climb at his side.

The air is thin, each breath a rasp,
But the summit is nearly in his grasp.
"To the summit and safely home"
The repeated mantra becomes a drone.
A few more inches, a few more feet,
An iron will won't admit defeat.
And then he stands with axe raised high,
Surrounded only by clouds and sky.
The spirits softly fade away,
And he stands alone; just for today.
He looks down at the clouds below
And other peaks clothed in snow.
He takes the moment as his own
In a world only gods have known.
"To the summit and safely home".

LAND TRUST

Urban sprawl!
Waste it all!
Is this how we will treat the land?
Destroy it all by our own hand?
The land does stretch from shore to shore,
It's just so much and nothing more.
Keep this land wild and free,
Not for you and not for me.
But for the ones who follow you.
For wolf and fox and otter too.
Waste not! Want not! Save a tree
For open space where all are free.
It's only ours to hold in trust;
To safeguard it is a must.
Pristine beauty for all to see,
A gift to the future from you and me.

THE CALL TO PRAYER

I want to hear the call to prayer;
An unseen force draws me where
Stately minarets rise so high
They pierce the azure desert sky.
The bazaar with its colorful sights and sounds
And veiled women making the rounds
Of stalls with spices, cloth and tea
Call like a siren song to me.
I want to join the nomad band
As it wanders across the dune filled land
To find a sheltered place to stay,
Following an ancient, unchanged way.
We'll wander across the wadis and dunes
To rest in the shade of an oasis at noon.
Then continue on under a darkening sky
Until we reach the caravanserai,
Where I veil my face so none can see
This person who is really me.
Hidden from each casual glance
While stars above spin and dance,
Like tiny gems of reflected light
Strewn across the velvet night.
Then incense burned to ward off Jinn
The horses and camels are saddled again.
The morning light is kissing the sky
When we depart the caravanserai.
This is where I long to be,
Travelling across this dune filled sea
To the next oasis and then
I'll hear the call to prayer again
Ringing out singsong over the land
And drawing me home across he sand.

In Native American tradition members of the weasel family are known for seeking out secrets. They hunt silently and can slip into small spaces. Weasels, fishers and mink teach us to be silent and observe. Many things will be communicated to us if we just watch and wait.

FISHER-CAT

Fisher-cat,
Weasel-like,
She looks Like that.
Seal brown fur,
I look
At her,
She looks
At me.
We watch
Each other Quietly.

My heart
Is pounding,
Can she
Hear?
Small dark eyes
Show no
Fear.

I look
At her,
She looks
At me.
Then bounds
Away,
Silently.

AIR

ALLAHU AKBAR

الله اكبر

MUEZZIN CALLING
BEDU FALLING
TO THEIR KNEES
IN THE SAND.

CAMEL BRAYING,
TASSELS SWAYING,
BEDU PRAYING,
"ALLAHU AKBAR."

DUN SAND BLOWING,
RED SUN GLOWING,
BEDU KNOWING,
"ALLALUH AKBAR."

SHADES

These others i have known before
from long ago and days of yore
they walk with me with silent stride
always, always by my side.
the harem girl with eyes of brown
the sun and moon adorn her gown
The armored knight with cross of red
his destrier being quietly led
across the endless dunes of sand
his focus on a distant land.
The Saracen on his Arab mare,
Is he real? Is he there?
He gallops across a desert sea
One that only I can see.
The midwife with her bitter brew
She made us drink, me and you
She saved me from a fevered grave.
When I was once a child, yet brave
I held her hand and called her name
But nothing now is still the same.
She doesn't turn, she doesn't see
Does she still remember me?
I wonder if I will see them when
I'm a shade -- just like them

FAIRY RING

Don't step inside the fairy ring
Where the fairies dance and sing
As they frolic through the night
Dancing with such wild delight.
Titania with her flowered gown
And Oberon with golden crown
Oversee each wild delight
Laughing, dancing through the night.
Step inside this fairy ring
Where the fairies dance and sing
And you'll join in and dance around
You can't resist the magic sound
Of music played on fairy flutes
By the old oak's gnarled roots.
Music played beyond compare
By fairy maids with golden hair.
Stardust sparkles in the air
And moonbeams dance everywhere.
Then Oberon blows his golden horn
To sound the coming of the morn.
And when the sun is overhead
And night's dark shadows all have fled
You will think it's still today
But many years have passed away.
For every hour in fairy time
Could be a decade in yours and mine.
Where you were once young and free
You will now an old mn be.
So don't be drawn by wild delights
On those quite, moonlit nights.
Don't step inside the fairy ring
Where for years you'll dance and sing.

FORTUNE TELLER

The priestess looks into the flame,
A flickering image, perhaps a name.
She casts the rune stones on the floor;
Maybe these will tell her more.

The crescent moon drawn on her brow,
She sees the shadowy image now.
Fleeting like dreams in the night
That fade with dawn and the light.

She sees what others cannot see,
Things still hidden from you and me.
She sees what mortal eyes can't see;
Things yet to come, things that will be.

The words she speaks come from another,
The one her people call "Great Mother".
A voice which speaks but makes no sound;
Magical words cast on the ground.

Tell me priestess what they say
Before the night gives way to day.
Tell me what will come be;
The future only you can see.

The words she speaks are soft and low,
Words that in my heart I know.
The future that is yet to be
Is one that only I can see.

MAGIC CARPET RIDE

Come take a magic carpet ride

And sit right here by my side.

Like a Rajah on his throne,

We'll fly away to realms unknown.

To the land where magic lives

And make-believe's what really is.

Stars will spin and moons will glow;

Galaxies will ebb and flow.

Tomorrow will be yesterday;

Aladdin's lamp will light the way.

Jinn will grant us wishes three,

So come and take a ride with me!

MEDITATION

Am I here? Is it today?
Or am I somewhere far away?
Walking through a forest green,
It's ancient oaks long unseen
By any but a chosen few,
The mossy path still wet with dew.
Or am I on a mountain high,
Where I can reach and touch the sky?
And there upon the rocky side
That falls away to canyons wide,
I hear the eagle's haunting cry
And hawk and I see eye to eye.
Or am I somewhere in the past?
A temple where a priestess casts
Runestones on a smooth-worn floor
While I wait to see what more
The silent stones will have to say
Before I quickly turn away.
And now I see a gilded door
That leads out to a sandy shore.
A hidden door, that has no key,
A door that just my mind can see.
It opens to the other side,
With azure sky and ocean wide.
And as I walk along the sand,
A stranger comes and takes my hand.
And leads me to where I can see
That it's today and I am me.

THE MESSENGER

In Native American folklore the hawk is a guardian and a messenger.

Brother hawk, I see you there,
Drifting, drifting through the air.
Tell! What message do you bring,
Silently, on feathered wing?
Magical, mystical bird of prey,
With eyes to see way past today.
Riding thermals, rising high,
A silhouette against the sky.

Ancient sentinel, power and grace,
Crossing the boundaries of time and space,
Your message now is loud and clear
Only for those with ears to hear.
But silently we turn away,
Focused only on today.
Brother eagle hears you though,
Circling, circling, oh, so slow.

He hears the voices in his head,
Of you and others, now long dead.
They tell him how it used to be,
They tell him things he doesn't see.
His eyes look past the present view,
To all that's old and all that's new.
And as he circles high above,
He looks with hate; he looks with love.

He hates the changes man has wrought,
These aren't the ways he was taught.
Taking what he needs to live,
This senseless waste he can't forgive.
He sees way back to years ago,
Seeing then it would be so.
But as he tips his wing and banks,
He gives a silent prayer of thanks.
For he loves the mountains, wild and free,
That stretch away to kiss the sea.
And he can rise above it all,
And still can hear the North Wind call,
To come where glaciers spread so far
And North is marked with a steady star,
Where eagles see with second sight
And cold blue flames light up the night.
He leaves man's folly all behind
To go where icy rivers wind
Across the tundra thick with snow,
To follow where his heart will go.
But brother hawk you chose to stay,
To try and show us all the way.
You call your message loud and clear,
And hope that we have ears to hear.

MUSE

My muse has left,
She dared not stay.
She oh so softly
Slipped away.

Will she return?
I do not know.
But how I hope
And wish it so!

ON HIGH

Come stand on this mountaintop with me
And see what only the gods can see.
Hills and valleys blue with haze
Stretch beyond your farthest gaze.

Silver streams tumble down,
Too far away to hear the sound.
Cotton clouds go drifting by;
Fat, white ships that sail the sky.

Feel the wind blow through your hair,
Feel the bite of the frigid air.
You'll see today will fade from view
And you'll see things few others do.

Things long past and yet to be,
These and more are things you'll see.
So come and stand with clouds and sky,
Come stand with me, here on high.

SHADOWS

See my heart speak.
Hear my eyes see.
Ancient shadows from the past,
Walk softly alongside of me.

Gently guiding,
Maybe chiding,
Speaking to the heart of me.

SHAPE-SHIFTING

I shape-shift once and I am there,
A high born priestess with long dark hair.
I close my eyes and change again
And a hawk soars over the canyon rim.
Then I might become a bee,
A hive of honey in an old dead tree.
Or maybe a drop of precious rain
Falling on the arid plain.

I change again to a panther sleek,
Roaming the jungle on velvet feet.
Perhaps a single stalk of grain
Or chestnut horse with flaxen mane
Galloping through the desert wide,
Sturdy bay colt at my side.
I shape-shift once, then yet again
And where I end I now begin.

Written for Raymond DiGregorio who spent many hours watching the birds at his feeders before he too would head South for the winter.

SNOWBIRD

Snowbird cheeping,
Softly creeping,
Round my feeder
In the snow.

Titmice flutter,
As I shudder,
At the wind
Across the snow.

Brown dove sighing,
Gently prying,
One more seed
From out the snow.

Wild geese flying,
Mournful crying,
Heading South
Escape the snow.

Snowbird dreaming,
As I'm scheming,
To follow where
The wild geese go.

THE BOOK OF TIME

The book of time is open to thee
So you can see,
So you can see.
Come! Take a
Look with me!

A heavy tome with edges gold; Oh, so very old!
It's yellowed pages, cracked and torn;
It leather binding soft and worn.
And lettered down it's heavy spine
Only the one word –TIME

But few can read
Or feel the need
To take a look
At this old book.
It tells of ancient floods and fires
It tells of hate
And man's desires.
And those who dare
To take a peek
Will surely find all they seek.

THE LACE MAKER

She weaves a web of silken thread
A pattern only in her head.
Her fingers fly with ease and grace;
Delicate stories made of lace.
Each subtle shape that she makes
A way that she communicates.
A language without words or sound
Growing slowly round by round.
She sits for hours in her small space
Weaving words of graceful lace.

TOUCHING THE SKY

Come stand with me where we can see
Across the hills to eternity.
Come stand with me where we can be
Like the hawk, so wild and free.
Where we can stand and be so high
It feels like we could touch the sky.

To look out at the endless view
Of valleys green and skies so blue
They dazzle with their changing hue.
Then look again and all is new.
As we stand and turn around,
Everything changes without a sound.

And we can see a thousand years
Rolling back with joy and tears.
And we can hear them walking by –
Others who have climbed so high,
To feel the wind against their face
And feel the beauty of this place.

They labored up this rocky trail,
This mountaintop their holy grail,
And maybe said a silent prayer
To the gods residing where
Only those who climb so high
Can reach right out and touch the sky.

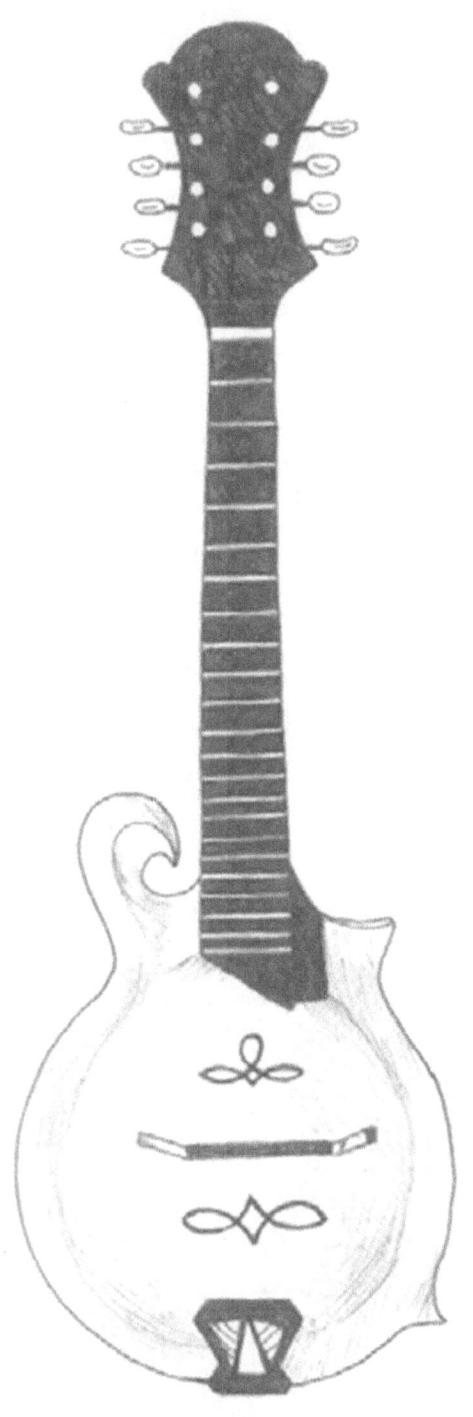

TROUBADOUR

In the Middle Ages wandering minstrels crossed the land singing stories of love and tales of great deeds. They often wandered from one royal court to another.

Troubadour! Sing some more!

Of the bygone days of yore.

Sing to me of Castles old;

And the knights, were they bold?

Tell me tales of love, I pray;

Was it only yesterday

That you wandered o'er the land,

Dusty harp in you hand?

Or was it many years ago

That all this was really so?

Why does that melody you sing

Have a faint, familiar ring?

Troubadour! Come sing to me!

Sing the stories I can see!

VESPERS

I sit in this holy place,
All around me sacred space.
And as the rain softly falls
Gently on these hallowed halls,
Soft sweet chanting fills the air
And banishes all earthly care.
Flickering candles dimly show
Hooded faces in the glow.
Ancient stones arching 'round
Softly echo the haunting sound.
As swirls of incense fill the air,
A sandaled foot upon the stair
Reminds me of another day,
Another lifetime far away.
And once again I am there,
A cowled monk at evening prayer.

THE WHEEL OF THE YEAR

On Solstice night
Call back the light.
Holly King, Oak King
Now will fight.
This is Yule,
Oak King will rule,
Bringing the light
With his strength
And his might.
The Yule Log burns.
The Wheel turns.

As Beltane comes round
The Wheel of the Year,
The days are no longer
So dark and so drear.
The King Stag rules
Till the young one is grown;
At Beltane the seeds
Of life are sown.
The Maiden for her consort
Yearns,
The Wheel turns.

On Midsummer day
Smell the new mown hay.
The byres are filled,
The fields are tilled.
Hang Rowan sprigs over the door,
Evil will enter nevermore.
Now is the year's longest day.
The meadows are gay
With flowers and ferns.
The Wheel turns.

Gather now your ears of corn,
Bright and early Lammas morn.
In the Wheel of the year
The harvest is here.
And now we know
We reap what we sow.
John Barleycorn must die
Beneath the summer sky.
It's the lesson one learns
As the wheel turns.

On Samhain Eve
For the dead we grieve.
The leaves have long
Been gold and red;
The "veil is thin",
Or so it's said.
The embers die
And witches fly.
The moon rides high
In an ebony sky.
The days are cold,
The year grows old.
And the Wheel turns.
The Wheel turns.

FIRE

CRUSADE

Pope Urban II called for the First Crusade at Clermont, France in 1095. Due to the law of primogeniture, landless younger sons were wreaking havoc around Europe, fighting one another. Urban would channel this energy and direct their aggression to a common cause. Jerusalem was in Moslem hands and by fighting to recapture the Holy City for the Church all sins would be forgiven. The response was overwhelming. Approximately 40,000 left Europe, two-thirds dying of disease, thirst, starvation and battles with the enemy before they ever reached Jerusalem. Then battle turned to slaughter, the Crusaders killing Moslem, Jew and Christian, until the knights rode in blood up to the horse's knees. Urban had unleashed a horror that did not end until the Marmaluke General Baibars rode out of Egypt and reclaimed the Holy Land in the thirteenth century.

Destrier = large war-horse of the Franks, bred to carry knights into battle.
Godfrey = Godfrey de Bouillon, leader of the First Crusade

"Take the Cross". I heard Urban say
As I stood at Clermont that summer day.
"Purge your sins and fear of Hell,
By saving Jerusalem from the Infidel!"

So "On to Jerusalem!" we raised the cry,
To fight in God's name; an honor to die.
We didn't know then, as we rode out that day,
Three years of hardship would bar the way.
As our army crossed this desert land
With endless miles of burning sand;
With thirst and sweat and scorching heat;
My faithful destrier slain for meat.

Pope Urban lied, with tales to tell
Of fighting against the Infidel.
Our sins are purged, that may be,
But Hell is as far as my eye can see.

And then the Holy City ahead,
Two thirds of my brethren already dead.
But driven by greed and glory and hate,
We stormed the city through Damascus Gate.

Then with blood-lust filling my heart,
We tore the Holy City apart.
And though I fought by Godfrey's side,
In the blood and dirt of battle I died.

Struck down by a mighty Saracen sword;
Did he also heed his God's word?
All my courage for naught that day
As I felt my life slowly slip away.

And as the streets flowed with red,
Moslem, Jew and Christian were dead.
Blood as high as a bridle rein;
But it was done "in God's Name."

The area called "The Horns of Hattin" for the two rocky peaks that rise over the desert near the Sea of Galilee was the scene of one of the bloodiest battles of the Crusades. The weak and unpopular King of Jerusalem, Guy de Lusignan, was urged to attack the city of Tiberias by the arrogant and ambitious Master of the Templars, Girard de Ridefort.

Near exhaustion from marching in the July sun with no water, they made camp on a plateau below the Horns of Hattin. During the night, they were surrounded by the armies of Saladin and as dawn broke and the Saracens attacked, the Crusaders' fate was sealed.

THE BATTLE OF THE HORNS OF HATTIN

July 4, 1137

King Guy, the weak
Said *"Let's retreat!"*
Girard said
"I'd rather be dead
Then turn my back.
Let's attack!
At dawn we ride!
God's on our side!"

This wrong advice King Guy did bide;
Not strong enough to turn aside
The ever overwhelming tide.
"Walking dead" they were then,
Heading for the Horns of Hattin.
Saladin's men, set to attack,
Surrounded them both front and back.
"A bloody massacre" it was said
With 20,000 Crusaders dead,
Or fallen into Saracen hands
And sold as slaves in other lands.
The Holy Land was now at last
Slipping from the Crusaders' grasp.
Saladin's army an avenging hand
Sweeping clean it's ancient land.
The Battle of Hattin was lost;
Pride and arrogance not worth the cost
Of corpses strewn across the land,
Covered by the blowing sand.
Now the bones are long laid bare;
Turned to dust in the desert air.
The Horns of Hattin mute witness bear
To all the lives that ended there.
And only the shades of many dead men
Will linger here at the Horns of Hattin.

OTHERS

Who are the ones
Who walk with me,
By my side
So silently?

The wounded knight
With face so grim
He struggles on
To purge his sin.
An endless quest
This Holy Land.
That, or die
On burning sand.
A shining sword
Now dark with rust,
Sun-bleached bones
Turned to dust.

I turn my head
Again, and see
The caravan, can
They see me?
Slowly, slowly, they
Pass me by
Under the glare of
A white hot sky.
One foot forward
Then another
A slow, sweet rhythm
Like no other.

Moving on for
Endless days,
Listen now!
A camel brays.

The village woman
From the square
Burned as a witch,
Her bones laid bare.
She reaches out
To touch my hem.
She is also
One of them.
Remember me!
She seems to say,
Or all for naught
That horrid day
When I died
So you might share
The ancient knowledge
That I bear.

Now I'm walking
Hand in hand
With a priestess
From a land
Ancient when
He Sent the Flood.
A land bathed in
Tears and blood.

She looks at me
And sweetly smiles,
I've been with her
These many miles.
Or is it years?
Centuries blurred
Through my tears.

Are these others
Here to stay
Or will they
Softly fade away?
Till only shadows
I will see
By my side,
So silently.

SPINNING WHEEL

Clack-clack; Clack-clack,
I hear the sound
Of the spinning wheel
Going round and round.
Am I here or am I *there*;
The sounds of silence
Fill the air.
The dungeon's dark,
No light, no air,
Am I here?
Or am I *there*?

Clack-clack, Clack-clack,
Is that the rack?
The creaking gears
Taking up the slack?
No, no, be calm
And do not fear;
It's just the
Spinning wheel I hear!

Clack-clack, Clack-clack,
Are those his boots
On the floor?
The executioner
Stands at my door.
His face is dark,
The light is dim;
"It's time" he says
When I look at him.
Then the image fades again
As I turn the wheel
And start to spin.

Clack-Clack, Clack-clack,
The memories come
Then fade away
Now I'm here,
And it's today.
But the whirr, the purr,
The soothing sound
Of the spinning wheel
Going round and round
Makes me wonder
Where I am
And if yesterday
Is back again.

Clack-clack, Clack-clack,
Hear the sound
Of the spinning wheel
Going round and round.

The Poor Knights of Christ of the Temple of Solomon (the Knights Templar) were an order of warrior monks founded in 1118 by Hughes de Payens to guard the pilgrims enroute to the Holy Land. They became the largest and most famous military order to fight in the Crusades, wearing the white mantle with the familiar red cross. Although vowed to poverty the order itself became extremely rich and was accused of learning occult secrets from the Saracens against whom they were fighting. Their wealth and power inspired envy and fear. They were accused of heresy and arrested on October 13, 1307 by King Philip IV of France who had bullied the weak Pope Clement V into letting him proceed. Philip was financially in debt to the Templars and coveted the large holdings of land they had acquired in France. The last of the grand masters, Jacques de Moley was burned at the stake by Philip in 1314. Legend says that as the flames were lit de Moley called out the innocence of his Order and that Philip would stand for judgment, within the year, at the throne of God. That same year Philip was killed in a riding accident, fulfilling de Moley's prophecy.

POOR KNIGHTS OF THE TEMPLE

"Poor Knights of Christ" they were called then,
Hughes de Payens and eight good men;
To guard the pilgrims 'cross burning sand
As they made their way to the Holy Land.

Poverty, chastity, obedience would they vow
And their numbers grew to thousands now.
Monks bearing arms in Christ's Name
"The Knights of the Temple" they became.

Warrior monks with mantles white
They came to the Holy Land to fight.
To die a martyr's death for Him
And win the city of Jerusalem.

Fierce as a lion, a gentle lamb,
A fighting monk with sword in hand.
Hair cropped short and dusty beard,
A Christian knight that all feared.

Storming heaven with his sword,
Prepared to die for Christ the Lord.
Twenty thousand knights in battle fell
To wrest His land from the Infidel.

But untold secrets they learned as well
Before the Holy City fell.
Knowledge of alchemy and hermetic thought;
Esoteric knowledge the Saracens taught.

Word of their knowledge and power spread;
"A vast hidden treasure" it was said.
Envious eyes turned toward them
As they rode home from Jerusalem.

A pope and a king did covet their wealth
And laid their plans with evil and stealth.
Heresy! Blasphemy! Their slanderous cry,
Accusing all Templars, now doomed to die.

Arrested and charged that October day,
"Poor Knights" led by Jacques de Moley.
Tortured and burned for the greed of a king
Who on his own head a curse did bring.

At the throne of God he stood in a year,
Devine judgment brought to bear.
The Templar's treasure was never found,
The remaining brethren gone to ground.

Some say to Scotland with Robert the Bruce
To fight for freedom and honor and truth.
Where they vanished none can explain
But their legend lives in honor and fame.

TEMPLAR

Templar knight speak to me;
Tell me who you really be.
Did you guard the pilgrim grim,
On the dusty road to Jerusalem?
Or is your purpose yet untold;
The search for wealth, the search for gold.
Is it knowledge arcane you seek,
Hermetic secrets, you dare not speak?
Tell me, knight, is it true?
Tell this heart that speaks to you.
Crusader knight with rosy cross,
What sacrifice did all this cost?

"Poor Knight of Christ" with wealth untold;
Some of it knowledge, some of it gold.
A monstrous price they made you pay
To jealous rivals on that black day.

Crusader knight, my heart is thine;
I feel your presence far across time.
Through the ages speak to me,
And tell me who you really be.

WARRIOR MONK

WARRIOR MONK WITH CROSS PF RED
THEY STRUCK YOU DOWN
THOUGHT YOU WERE DEAD.

BUT I HEAR YOU CALL
ACROSS ENDLESS SAND
IT ECHOES THROUGH THE
HOLY
LAND.

DID I RIDE WITH YOU
IN YEARS GONE BY?
DID I RAISE MY SWORD TO THE
INFIDEL'S CRY?

WITH CLINK OF ARMOR
AND CLASH OF STEEL
THE BURNING DESERT SUN
I FEEL.

WARRIOR MONK WITH
TALES TO TELL,
OF BLOOD AND DEATH ND THE
INFIDEL.

YOUR VOICE CALLS OUT
TO TOUCH ME HERE;
WHAT ANCIENT PAST DID WE
SHARE?

TELL ME KNIGHT WHO
WALKS WITH ME
DID I EVER RIDE WITH
THEE?

During the Inquisition millions of people were accused of witchcraft and burned at the stake. Many of these were harmless old women whose knowledge of midwifery, herbs and folk cures ran them amok of the established Church.

WISE WOMAN

Wise woman in your hut by the wood,
I ask for your help, I beg that you should
Weave me a spell; my love's gone astray;
I pray that you help me return him today.

Wise woman, wise woman, my goode-wife's abed;
Make me a potion, ere she be dead.
Brew me a cure and I'll thankful be;
Won't you please hurry and do this for me?

"Parsley and sage and rosemary too,
Will make a fine potion to keep your love true.
Dandelion, thistle and comfrey for sure,
I'll give the good lady a tea for her cure."

Wise woman help me, I know that you can,
We wish for a child, me and my man.
If this small favor you would do for me,
Then forever hereafter I will grateful be.

"Take this my child when the moon shows new
And drink it all down, this dark bitter brew.
The Goddess will grant you the child you desire,
To gladden your hearth as you sit by the fire."

Wise woman! Old woman! The cat by your door
Must be the Devil says old Father Moore.
Evil witch! Sorceress! Hear the crowd cry.
Lonely old woman condemned now to die.

Wise woman, wise woman consigned to the flame;
How could we do this, all in God's Name?
All the old knowledge now dead in the fire;
Who will be left to grant our desire?

WATER

UNKNOWN

Oh templar knight
It seems to me
Your raison d'etre
Could never be.
Nine men to guard
The Pilgrim road;
It seems to be
A heavy load.

Is your reason
Something more?
What brought you
To Outremer's shore?
Was arcane knowledge
Your hidden goal?
Knowledge that could
Risk your soul?

Or was it treasure
That you sought
And all the power
That it brought?
Or was it secrets
Of the grail?
The troubadours
Do tell that tale.

The rumors swirl
Across the years;
The truth obscured
By blood and tears.
Destroyed by
Envy, greed and fear,
Only an echo
Lingers here,
Of the men
Who rode to death
Across the desert's
Length and breadth
Would that I
Could see the past
And really know
The truth at atlas

ON TURNING EIGHTY-SIX

How did I so fast arrive at the great age of 86?
When only yesterday it seems was baseball,
Marbles, pick-up-sticks.
While the years are speeding up
And snow and ice do soon arrive
Right after rose and buttercup.
I'm slowing down
To look around.
I come to that great place in life
Where I can turn around and see
All the things along the way
That shaped the person known as "me."
And I am now unique, you see,
For things accomplished, heights attained,
That make me special, make me "me."
And I can conquer even more
Than in the days when I was young
Because of wisdom and of lore
Gleaned along life's winding way.
So come and celebrate with me
Those dreams accomplished
And also those still yet to be.
For I have learned so much, much more
Then in the days of "pick-up-sticks"
So even though I'm stiff and sore
I'm proud to say I'm 86!

Written for Christian John Petersen

ODE TO A VIKING

You who gives your heart to me
Let me shelter in your lee.
So I can bear a stormy gale
As the seas of life we sail.
My chains are yours and yours are mine,
While joy and sorrow intertwine.
We'll travel far or bide a while,
My hand in yours with every mile.
Your love is all the world to me
As I shelter in your lee.

TELL ME

"Don't love me", you say
Well, show me the way.
Love's blind and I cannot see.

Tell the sun not to rise
And stand still in the skies,
You can't stop this folly in me.

Tell the hawk not to fly
So far and so high,
Tell the wild hart not to run free.

When these things you can say,
Then tell me the way
That I can stop loving thee.

HE

When he turns around, I see
His eyes look in the soul of me.
The fates ordained I cannot flee;
Some things just are meant to be.

The years go by so swift, so fast;
This love was surely meant to last.
My love is strong, my heart is bold;
He is now growing old.

But still though all the years, I see
His eyes look in the soul of me.
To memories of ages past, or maybe
Lives still yet to be.
My love will cross eternity.

UNVEILED

Tell me that you love me true
And I will tell the same to you.
The path we walk is rough and steep
But hold my hand and love will keep
Me by your side along this way,
So hearts may speak what words can't say.

Once before I walked with thee
My veiled face none could see.
I walked behind three steps or more,
Until we reached the hareem *door.*
Only then my lips to kiss,
Only then such worldly bliss.

But now you hold me close to you
And tell me that you love me too.
And though the path is ever steep,
Your hand in mine will always keep
Me by your side in this new day,
So hearts will speak what words can't say.

SEA SONG

The slap of the sails, the creak of the stays,
The sounds of a sailboat, well under way.

Rocking gently as we move along,
The wind is singing a sweet siren song.

Endless blue water stretches away
And up from the bow a soft, salt spray.

The sun and the wind are strong at my back.
Filling the sails and leaving no slack.

I take up the line and turn hard a lee,
Just the sails, the sun, the wind and me.

VERNAL POOL

A vernal pool is quite a place,
Not here or there in time or space.
Gone tomorrow, here today,
Just to visit, not to stay.

Salamanders, frogs and things
With tiny lacy, gossamer wings
Come for a while but not to stay;
They'll be back another day.

Another spring when nights are cool
And soft, warm rain fills the pool;
Before the blazing summer sun
Signals that their time is done.

And as the pool fades away
To be reborn another day;
The uplands beckon for a time
And they'll seek out a drier clime.

But when spring thaws the winter snow,
Somehow in their hearts they know
Their pool is waiting cool and deep,
Roused from it's winter sleep.

Back from another place
Far outside of time and space.
It's fleeting beauty here today,
For a while, but not to stay

GODDESS

I hear the Goddess calling,
Where from – I do not know.
I feel her voice around me,
I hear it sweet and low.

I hear the Goddess calling,
A siren song to me.
Oh how I long to follow,
I hear but cannot see.

I hear the Goddess calling
Come, learn the Ancient Ways.
Come, taste the fruit of knowledge,
Seeds sown in olden days.

I seek to find this Goddess,
To learn what I must know;
I search in the far mountains,
Still covered white with snow.

I seek her in the breezes
That blow gently through my hair.
I search along the riverbank;
It seems she isn't there.

I seek her in the Magick
Of spell and candlelight;
I search in the meadows
On a clear and moonlit night.

I yearn to find the Goddess
In those myths from long ago,
And learn from her the secrets
Which all wise women know.

I hear the Goddess calling
As she whispers soft, I see,
To seek without is folly,
The Goddess is in Me.

IMAGES

I see as in a mirror, darkly;
Reflections I can barely see.
Images of ages past,
Fleeting and not meant to last.
Like softly sifting desert sand,
Swept across an ancient land.
I see as in a mirror, darkly;
Images of long ago.
Glimpses of an unseen land,
Touched by an unseen hand.

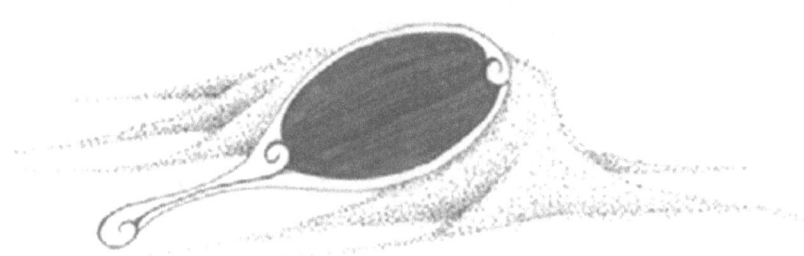

REFLECTIONS

REFLECTIONS

I live my life in minor key
That slightly off-beat melody.

        Taunting,

                Daunting,

                        Sweetly haunting,

                                  Reflections of the inner me.

I live my life in minor key
That slightly off-beat melody.

        Taunting,

                Daunting,

                        Sweetly haunting,

                                  Reflections of the inner me.

HECATE

Hecate is the Crone (the grandmother or old wise woman) aspect of the triple Goddess. The Goddess manifests in three different forms – Maiden, Mother and Crone. Hecate is the ruler of Magick. Her place is the crossroads and her time is the dark of the moon.

Hecate, Hecate, Grandmother, Crone!
I come to the crossroads,
I come here alone.
I leave you an offering,
Here, in this place,
In the dark hour of night,
When the moon hides her face.
Hecate, Hecate, come show me your ways;
Secrets I've known in much older days.
Hecate, Hecate, this prayer I do say,
At the crossroads in darkness
So you'll light the way.

Hecat, Hecate, Dark Mother of mine!
I hear you, I feel you reach across time.
Your hand on my shoulder, my heart hears you say,
"Come, follow me now, I'll show you the way".

SOUL

The soul is Love, is Light, is Life;
Bound to me in earthly strife.

Learn lessons well it says to me,
For only then will you be free
From the wheel of Death and Birth,
That binds you to this lowly Earth.

Learn lessons well it says to me;
And then you will be truly free.

SPIRIT

In the fall of the year when days grow short it's believed that the veil between this world and the other world grows thin and those that we love who have passed away are closer then at any other time. This is one reason why Samhain (or Halloween) and All Souls' Day are celebrated on October 31 and November 1.

Dearest shade, are you here?
Out of sight but somewhere near?
Hidden from all human view,
Behind the veil 'tween me and you.
Other realms have claimed you now,
But when the veil is thin, somehow
I feel your presence ever near
To comfort me and ease my fear.

I hear your voice so soft and low,
A shadow in the candle's glow.
A well loved step upon my stair,
If only I could glimpse you there.
A different form from what you wore
When you walked the earth before
Death took you to the other side
And left me here alone to bide.

But often in dusk's dim light,
When the day gives way to night
And boundaries softly blur away
So night's not night and day's not day,
I feel your presence by my side;
Do the portals open wide?
For one brief moment do I see
You standing here right next to me?

Wyrd is the Anglo-Saxon word for the Old Norse "Urd" or fate. Fate was controlled by three sister goddesses who spun the web of humankind's destiny. Clothos spun the thread of life, Lachesis wove and measured it and Atropos cut it at life's end. It was believed that anything that one did to interfere with fate would return to you and in some cultures it is still believed that whatever you send out, for good or evil, will return times three.

THE WEB OF WYRD

To make magic happen
Takes power and thought,
And then there's the spells
One must be taught.
If I had this power
You think I'd be feared,
If I could then tremble
The Web of Wyrd?

Then I would make
All the demons quake,
With notions and potions
All which I would make;
With "words of power"
For each sigil and sign,
And incense smoke
To focus my mind.

With crystal ball
The spirits I'd call,
To tell what I wish to know.
With robes and wand
And herbs that I grow,
I'd really be ready
To put on a show.

But it's what's in your heart
And not in your head
That makes magick happen,
Or so it's been said.
And for good or for bad
All these things that you do
When you tremble the Web
Will come right back to you.

WISHES

"If wishes were horses" my mother would chide;
"If wishes were horses, then beggars would ride."
"Wishing and hoping won't make it so"….
Oh yes, it will! This much I know!

Make a wish upon that star
And suddenly you're somewhere far
Away from all that's here today.
Somewhere new and far away.

Wish upon the candles' glow;
Wish real hard before you blow.
The universe will surely hear,
Your wish comes true, within the year.
So make a wish and follow your dreams,
For nothing is really as it seems.
"And if wishes were horses….." my mother would say.
So I'll get on my horse and ride away!

Written for Christian John Petersen whose sloop "Dragonfire"
took him to many far away places.

HERE THERE BE DRAGONS

A Viking ship cuts through the wave,
Her tired young captain is fearless and brave.
His long red hair is streaked with gold
And his pale blue eyes are young but old.
Weary of battles both won and lost,
Men sent to Valhalla whatever the cost.
He looks again at the dark restless sea.
"Here There Be Dragons" his charts decree.
"I'll be not afeared for a new land is there,
Just beyond the dragon's lair.
A new land is there at the edge of the sea,
A new land is there and it's calling to me"

Centuries pass and in this new land,
A sloop called Dragonfire sails away from the stand.
A rampart dragon, breathing red flame,
Adorns her sail and proclaims her name.
A flag unfurls in the now stiff breeze.
"Here There Be Dragons" it's message decrees.
And as the young captain turns his head,
His light brown hair is streaked with red.

His pale blue eyes are young but old,
A modern day Viking but no less bold
Then when he lived in a time before,
When the world was ruled by a God named Thor,
And Valkyries rode wildly across the sky,
Bringing to Valhalla all those who die.
Those young old eyes look across the sea.
"Here There Be Dragons and they're calling me."

www.ingramcontent.com/pod-product-compliance
Lightning Source LLC
Chambersburg PA
CBHW030501130626
46549CB00007B/2816